BORONAHHMR.
ART + DESIGN

Bauhaus

To Abstraction & the Poppet,
and to the "first years"

THIS IS A CARLTON BOOK

Text and design copyright © 2000 Carlton Books Limited

This edition published by Carlton Books Limited 2000
20 Mortimer Street
London
W1N 7RD
www.carltonbooks.com

A CIP catalogue for this book is available from the British Library

ISBN 1 84222 013 6

Executive Editor: Sarah Larter
Design: Zoe Mercer
Picture research: Catherine Costelloe
Production: Garry Lewis

Printed and bound in Dubai

Bauhaus

JUDITH CARMEL ARTHUR

This little book has been composed as a primer on the place of the

Bauhaus in twentieth-century design culture. It sets out to introduce some of the complex parameters of a subject on which there is a growing amount of well-documented research.

When the German architect Walter Gropius was approached in 1915 by the Belgian architect-designer Henry Van de Velde — then Director of the School of Applied Arts in Weimar — to be his future successor, neither man could have envisaged the controversial impact Gropius' school would later have. The Bauhaus has been called the most influential, as well as notorious, art school of the twentieth-century. It became a nerve centre for some of the most utopian ideologies and temperaments of its day.

Despite its brief fourteen-year history, its mere 1250 students, and its critically small contribution to the century's repertoire of material artefacts, its reputation remains beguiling to each new generation. Its tangible achievements in art educational theory and practice were formidable, establishing the canons of modern design education. The story of the Bauhaus is a history in brief of the emergence of modern design and of the strained relationships between art and machine technology. The discourses which were played out there revealed the laboured emergence of a uniquely twentieth-century design aesthetic.

The Bauhaus Faculty comprised a virtual "who's who" of contemporary modernist practitioners. Between the foundation of the school in 1919 and its closure in 1933 the Bauhaus staff included the Hungarian architect and designer, Marcel Breuer; Ludwig Mies van der Rohe, German architect and former apprentice to Peter Behrens, who had originally practised in a reticent nineteenth-century neo-classical style; the Swiss architect Hannes Meyer who assumed the directorship of the Bauhaus at Gropius' departure in 1928; László Moholy-Nagy, a former law student in Budapest who became one of the school's most provocative educationalists and constructivist practitioners; Johannes Itten, a Swiss designer and so-called

BAUHAUS

"mystic pedagogue" who was also a disciple of oriental philosophy and religion; Paul Klee, a former member of the German Expressionist group *Der Blaue Reiter* in Munich and a somewhat detached devotee of principles of harmonious composition; and Wassily Kandinsky, a Russian painter who had also been a former member of *Der Blaue Reiter*, and who advocated creative improvisation and "subjectless" art. He abandoned a teaching post at the acclaimed Vkhutemus School in Moscow to join the Bauhaus in 1922.

Essentially a state-funded art school, the history of the Bauhaus was tumultuous. Its perceived socialist tendencies and radical ethos of the Bauhaus were considered inimical by local authorities, particularly in the aftermath of Germany's 1918 Socialist Revolution, and the school was forced to move from Weimar to Dessau in 1925. When Gropius became disillusioned and resigned his directorship in 1928, he was succeeded by the intellectual Marxist Hannes Meyer who ran the Bauhaus until Mies van der Rohe took over in 1931. But again an apprehensive local government was made uneasy, and in 1932 Mies moved the school to Berlin where in the following year it was permanently closed by the Nazis who remained unconvinced of the values of modernism.

Originally called the Staatliches Bauhaus Weimar, the school was founded by Gropius in 1919 as an integration of the Weimar Academy of Fine Art (Sächsische Hochschule für Bildende Kunst) and the Weimar School of Applied Arts (Sächsische Kunstgewerbeschule). Today it is simply referred to as the *Bauhaus*, a term conceived by Gropius, combining the German verb *bauen* – to build – with the noun *Haus*. Although not precisely translatable, the word *Bauhaus* — roughly meaning "house for building" — reflects the idealism of it's founder's vision.

The term was essentially a metaphor for Gropius' belief in the theory of the *Gesamtkunstwerk*, the "total work of art" in which design became the synthesis of all the arts and crafts under the umbrella of architecture. There was a quasi-religious notion here of

BAUHAUS

design as a redemptive power in its own right; a radical facilitator within the context of a nation morally and economically defeated by the First World War. Design, Gropius maintained, could reshape a better, more integrated and ultimately democratic German society.

The Bauhaus *Manifesto* and *Programme* of 1919 formulated Gropius' initial priorities. His first concern was to establish architecture as the dominant design forum. The second sought to undermine traditional hierarchies by elevating the status of crafts skills to a level commensurate with fine art, while the third aim recalled the doctrines of the Deutsche Werkbund, an organization founded in Munich in 1907 which looked to "the improvement of industrial products through the combined efforts of artists, industrialists and craftsmen". Gropius wrote

“THE ULTIMATE **AIM**OF ALL creative activity IS THE **BUILDING”**

evoking an Arts and Crafts heritage and nodding to John Ruskin's notion that the medieval cathedral signified collaboration and integration of the arts; architecture represented the unification of all design and arts and crafts practices.

Although architecture was not initially taught at the Bauhaus, this romantic inflection characterized the school's curriculum which sought in practice to reintegrate the arts and crafts along medieval lines, educating designers, artists and craftspeople in a variety of convergent skills. Tutors were not "teachers" but "Masters", and students "journeymen"; concomitant titles rekindling ideals of specialist crafts skills and collaboration both in training and in execution.

An early and perhaps anomalous reflection of this approach was the overtly *völkish* Sommerfeld House (now destroyed) in Berlin, designed by Gropius in collaboration with Adolph Meyer in 1920 as the result of a commission to Gropius' private architectural practice. Constructed entirely of wood the structure reproduced a vernacular Germanic model of architectural ornament, form and collaborative processes. Its extensive carvings were executed by Joost Schmidt, an apprentice at the school. Marcel Breuer, later a Bauhaus Master, was one of the students who incorporated their varied contributions to the building into their examination portfolios. The project anticipated the Bauhaus building at Dessau which would come to be entirely fitted out with the school's designs. This approach was remarkably holistic, revealing a determined commitment to educational, if not aesthetic reform. It exemplified Gropius' initial predilection towards a craft ideal, as well as an entrenched dependence upon traditional crafts techniques as a guiding, healing force in national design.

Significantly, Gropius and Mayer had already created the early paradigm of modern functionalist architecture in the pre-war glass and steel Fagus Factory in Alfeld-an-der-Leine 1910–11, where many features of the future International Style were first realized. Gropius exploited cubic forms and the use of a glass curtain wall to produce transparent structure without apparent load-bearing support. It was a certain expression of rationalist industrial principles.

Gropius' apparent change in aesthetic direction at the later Sommerfeld House was undoubtedly a considered response to contemporary conditions. Wood was a comparatively plentiful resource in post-war Germany, while the commission provided a much needed opportunity for the school to further its interests in collaborative enterprise, in this instance relying upon crafts traditions and materials as unifying, culturally familiar models.

Gropius was assisted in realizing his second goal by the arrival in 1922 of László Moholy-Nagy who brought to the Bauhaus a strong commitment to the ideology of Russian Constructivism. As both a designer and a pedagogue, Moholy-Nagy aspired to eradicate fine art altogether in favour of a "modern" design which would assume a machine aesthetic thoroughly commensurate with socialist ideology.

Political issues aside, crucial cultural discourses about the comparative value of craft work were being played out at the Bauhaus. These encapsulated the problematic cultural transition from artistic and crafts-based artefact design to the industrial product. In the early years at Weimar, Gropius, at once a modernist and a maker, struggled to come to terms with a traditional craft ideal which promoted crafts process as an end in itself. Making was thought to carry the spirit of the maker. Throughout the school's history this crafts bias featured at the very core of the Bauhaus educational philosophy of "learning by doing", and the school thus maintained the humanism of a crafts ethic while aspiring, certainly after 1924, to production for industry.

The first year Preliminary Course, or *Vorkurs*, provided the model from which present day Foundation Courses are derived. Developed by Johannes Itten, it was mandatory for all students. The curriculum was theoretically based, comprising an exploration of the primary components of visual language: texture, colour, form, shape and materials. Students concentrated upon manipulating formal elements of abstraction, engaged in compositional studies and also in a variety of exercises familiarising them with the possibilities and limitations of individual materials. This programme was the essence of the school's educational structure and has since come to be known as the "Bauhaus method".

Because both Gropius and Itten believed that art could not be taught or learned, as such, the *Vorkurs* stressed the acquisition of craft and manual skill as a prerequisite for design. But, as Peter Dormer pointed out in *The New Ceramics* (1986) "Educationally, handwork was seen more as a way of sensitizing designers to materials than as an end itself. It is interesting that the ceramics workshops established in Weimar were not moved to Dessau ... "

Oddly, ceramics was dropped from the school's curriculum after 1925, despite a well-established European tradition of industrial production. It is possible that ceramics too conspicuously embodied the continuation of a hand-making aesthetic, coupled with the difficulty and expense of setting up production. An experienced industrial practitioner, not an artist, would have been required to oversee such a venture. Ironically, among the very first Bauhaus designs to be mass produced, Bogler's ceramic designs boasted a rationality and simplicity of form that influenced industrial ceramics in Germany throughout the 1930s.

One of the most crucial controversies to be played out at the Bauhaus was the discourse between fine art and craft. In the traditional aesthetic hierarchy, fine art had held a dominant position, overshadowing the materiality of crafts. Gropius was among those who called this hierarchic canon into question, promoting new opportunities for a heightened cultural status of design.

However, at Weimar fine artists were prevalent as tutors, clearly nurturing a bias towards aesthetic individualism. This soon became the antithesis of Gropius' convictions about, not the creative, but the design process.

Gropius had been influenced by the doctrines of the Deutsche Werkbund, and by one of their founders, Peter Behrens, having worked alongside Le Corbusier and Mies van der Rohe in Peter Behrens' architectural office in Berlin. Like Behrens, Gropius envisaged a marriage of design with industry as the most effective way of achieving high-standards in modern design. Thus in the *Manifesto*, his ambition was to establish an educational curriculum which would meet the needs of an emerging breed of industrial designer.

In order to achieve this result, a determined collaboration with the materials and processes of industry was necessary. Following the *Vorkurs*, further study at the Bauhaus was carried out in specialist workshops, including metal, pottery, stage design, carpentry, stained glass, typography, wall painting and, after 1924, architecture. As Sigrid Wortmann Weltge has pointed out, however, the only workshop to exist throughout the full life of the school was the weaving workshop, whose strength had developed from certain origins in the Weimar Bauhaus "women's department". The *Vorkurs* method continued to form the basis of educational procedure, while the workshops were meant to methodologically integrate the fine arts and crafts in an advanced curriculum, providing an innovative and dispassionate method of training.

However, the workshop Masters were themselves almost exclusively fine artists, and certainly during the Weimar years the approach was anything but dispassionate. Theories of form inspired by post-Cubist abstraction were favoured throughout the history of the school, but at Weimar there was an initial emphasis on the expressive language of abstraction, and on the emotive potential of an individual maker's use of visual language. The mood of the school reflected aesthetic individualism, a tendency which merged with a proclivity towards German Expressionism to which Gropius himself was not entirely unsympathetic. This was also encouraged by the presence of practising Expressionists such as Gerhard Marcks, the painter and set designer Oscar Schlemmer, Klee and Kandinsky.

Even in the Vorkurs, Johannes Itten stressed the role of intuition and personal self-discovery through abstraction. His emphasis on spiritualism in art, however, precipitated an internal controversy which altered the aesthetic direction of the school. Itten's insistence upon the individualistic, spiritual content of fine art, coupled with his eccentric behaviour (he wore a tunic, suggesting the same to his students in addition to a special diet and meditative breathing exercises) thrust him into the limelight of conservative Weimar, and into conflict with Gropius who invited him to leave the school in 1923.

Itten's departure brought about a new orientation at the Bauhaus, echoed in changes in the teaching staff. Moholy-Nagy and Josef Albers took over the *Vorkurs*, to which they brought the anti-art aesthetic of Russian Constructivism. They facilitated the modification of the course away from individual expression towards a more reasoned attitude to objective three-dimensional form. Moholy-Nagy emphasized the application of a machine aesthetic to real design, saying

"THE NEW PERCEPTUAL STRUCTURE IS FUNDED ON THE constituent ELEMENTS OF VISUAL REGISTRATION: DOT, LINE, extent, POSITION, DIRECTION."

Moholy-Nagy's abilities as a teacher were considerable. It has been suggested that his personal advocacy of a Constructivist ideology was largely responsible for changing the course of the Bauhaus after Itten's departure. As leader of the Preliminary Course he continued to focus on the development of progressive design principles through hands-on experimentation with materials, but focused on the machine as a metaphor for rational "modern" form. It symbolized standardized parts production, anonymous design and assembly. It produced industrial artefacts devoid of detail and valued for their generalized geometric configuration. These were "model forms" that signified the spirit of industrial progress and which were as "elegant" in their rationale as any correct mathematical equation. The blatant anonymity of the machine's making was equally inviting because it eradicated subjective expression and the necessary individualism of personal style. It talked of a collective, universal significance, a utopian faith in the modern age being brought about by post-war mass production.

At the same time both Klee and Gropius recognized the increasing necessity to educate students in terms of simplified principles suitable for mass production, moving more positively towards a synthesis of aesthetics with the machine. Klee had argued that the three basic units of all form were the circle, triangle and square, teaching that compositions were built by the variable relations between these "constructive" devices. His approach was essentially a reasoned, empirical one, emphasizing the objectivity of all visual vocabulary and suggesting the design process was to be a thoroughly rational one.

In 1923 Gropius delivered the seminal lecture entitled "Art and Technology: a New Unity" in which he attempted to re-evaluate the aesthetic direction of the school. He subsequently (1926) published "Principles of Bauhaus Production" summarizing the lecture and arguing that design must be linked with the machine in order to be "typical of our time".

At this ideological juncture the Bauhaus moved to Dessau. The new school saw as its mission the development of a "modern" design aesthetic. In this sense it was prepared to confront the twentieth-century head on, and to tackle the implicit questions raised by the post-World War One circumstances of material culture. These questions included many about the processes underlying design. How might industrial technology and materials be used in design, bringing the latter up to date with realities of the material world? What teaching methods were most appropriate, and which would best encourage experimentation with new technological materials?

To some extent Gropius' ideal of synthesis was realized in the workshops at Dessau, where individual specialists in both the crafts and arts taught side by side, each co-operating in other skills. Kandinsky had worked in the stained-glass studio, while Klee had applied his theories to textile design. The Bauhaus also saw some degree of collaboration in the workshops, even at Weimar. Although examples like that between the sculptor Gerhard Marcks and the ceramicist Otto Lindig were encouraged, such instances were infrequently realized.

The Dessau Bauhaus opened in 1926 in the now legendary, purpose-built complex designed by Gropius. Symbolically, the completed buildings were architecture in defence of pedagogy. Their furnishings, fixtures and fittings were designed and produced by members of the school, including both students and Masters. Planning priority focused upon principles of functional-ism, and the design was a further formulation of Gropius' statement at the Fagus Factory.

Cantilevering was foregrounded as both a practical response and a symbolic feature of emerging modernism. Each of the school's practical structures — administration, workshops, staff and student living quarters — was separately delineated, revealing a rationalist focus underlying the organization. The design overall can be interpreted as an expression of Gropius' belief in the unity of art and life, a unity dependent upon the clarity of each of its parts.

After its move to Dessau, the Bauhaus became known as a major protagonist of the so-called "machine" aesthetic which promoted simplification and standardization of form. Simplification of form had already been advocated by Itten during the *Vorkurs* where he discussed shapes which had been reduced to purely abstract configurations. After 1923, however, an earlier influence of the Dutch De Stijl movement resurfaced and this continued to have a marked effect on the direction of design at Dessau.

The De Stijl architect and theorist Theo Van Doesburg had visited Weimar in 1921–22 and had for a time published the influential *De Stijl* magazine there. The early influence of De Stijl at the Bauhaus is exemplified by Marcel Breuer's armchair of 1922, which forcefully relies on the intersection of verticals and horizontals, combined with the Bauhaus leitmotif of cantilevering to make its aesthetic point. Van Doesburg was one of the seminal influences on early modernism who argued the fundamental place of elementary form, especially the straight line, in a modernist art and design idiom. The De Stijl practitioner Gerrit Reitveld had produced the so-called "Berlin" chair acknowledged as a three-dimensional evocation of compositional theory based on the intersection of straight line and plane.

The arrival of the Bauhaus in Dessau represented a new attempt to more rigorously integrate art and design within the school's curriculum. This was now more possible as former students, for example Marcel Breuer, Gunta Stözl and Josef Albers, began to teach in the workshops. Their presence initiated a fresh emphasis upon production-based work and an increasingly objective application of basic form to design. In this way they began to achieve a synthesis of art with new technical possibilities, moving more effectively towards a new aesthetic for machine production. Even at Dessau, however, most workshop production methods remained crafts-based. Gropius' ideal of infusing the school with an art-into-industry bias was ever only partially achieved. His accent upon the workshops' fabrication of prototypes for industrial production resulted in quantitatively few manufactured products at the time, and eventually he became disillusioned.

The issue of prototypes for industrial manufacture has haunted the history of the Bauhaus. In *The Bauhaus Reassessed* (1985) Gillian Naylor showed how the workshops at Dessau were — at least ideologically — transformed into what Gropius called "laboratories" in which prototypes for machine production would be made. This change of direction has been considered the final blow to a crafts aesthetic at the school.

Critical scholarship has equally argued that despite Gropius' intentions to directly link design and design education with machine production, the workshops ultimately remained crafts-based in their procedures and were dependent upon traditional crafts products such as pots, tapestries, lamps and furniture. Although prototypes for manufacturing were produced, particularly once the school moved to Dessau, comparatively few Bauhaus prototypes ever reached the stage of commercial production.

Although receiving little popular recognition, the Dessau weaving workshop was, as Sigrid Wortmann Weltge has shown (1993), the exception. Gunta Stözl had been a student at the Bauhaus under Itten, when she went on to study with and assist after he left the Bauhaus in 1923. She, however, returned to Weimar in 1925, becoming a teacher in her own right and running the weaving workshop from 1926. Not only an expert weaver, Stözl also successfully designed prototypes for machine production. In the metal workshop under Moholy-Nagy, Wilhelm Wagenfeld produced prototypes, including that for a table lamp in 1923–24. When displayed at a trade fair in Leipzig in 1924 the prototype was, in retrospect ironically, criticized as resembling an inexpensive machine-made product. It became one of the metal workshop's success stories and was patented by the school. The design remains in production today. Marianne Brandt also worked in the metal workshop, and like Wagenfeld relied upon combinations of primary geometric forms in her design of new product prototypes. She applied a constructivist, formal aesthetic, like Wagenfeld, to the design of domestic artefacts, and in this way, pioneered a great selection of modern household ware. The fact that such prototypes were both made and finished by hand shows them to be part of a newly emerging design ideology. In contrast, Brandt's Kandem table lamp of 1927 is perhaps less stylistically elegant, but is a carefully planned manifestation of Gropius' aims of design for industry. Commercially hugely successful, it confirms the Dessau Bauhaus orientation towards the manufacturing ease of everyday objects.

The language of tubular steel has come to culturally signify the Dessau Bauhaus. It was incorporated into a series of prototypes by both Marcel Breuer and Mies van der Rohe, a number of which were put into production by Standard Möbel of Berlin, and by Thonet. These practitioners' experiments with tubular steel initiated new canons of furniture design.

The language of tubular steel as a design material was a supreme manifestation of the early century's discourse with the machine. It was a machine-made product, held to be especially characteristic of modernity and aesthetic anonymity. Various Bauhaus anecdotes arose regarding its application to furniture design. Marcel Breuer — perhaps the material's most adept practitioner — seems consistently to have been at the heart of these. Legend has it that his inspiration to employ tubular steel in furniture came from the handlebars of his new Adler bicycle. However the Junkers aircraft factory was also in Dessau and, in fact, nearby, and tubular steel was already employed there as a lightweight, structurally sound and cost effective material. Soon it was to become one of the most potent symbols of the Modernist agenda, valued for its tensile strength, ease and low cost of manufacturing, and its comparative simplicity in technological terms. It seemed to prove the viability of an aesthetic of anonymity .

Tubular steel was a paradigm of Dessau's rational approach to materials in opposition to individual expression, and manifest Gropius' focus on the responsibility of the designer during the very process of designing. Gestures such as this exemplified Gropius' desire to turn out designers comfortable with the modern world, as well as with modern and future means of production. He recognized that art and high design were remote from society in general, and thus embarked on an idealistic unification of creativity with contemporary production methods.

If, in reality, little was produced by the Bauhaus for actual manufacture, this is perhaps less significant in retrospect than the fact that the school was consistently a hot house for European-wide debate about the nature, status and means of design, and was ultimately highly contemporary in its democratic commitment to mass production. At the time, its immediate, material achievements were perhaps less noteworthy than the design-specific issues for which it served as a spirited provocateur. As Mies van der Rohe later said:

"THE BAUHAUS WAS NOT AN institution WITH A CLEAR PROGRAMME – IT WAS AN IDEA."

Walter Gropius believed that design should ideally evolve from a humanistic approach, and maintained that design's ability to respond in both form and process to the social and economic necessities of society was fundamental. He argued that the designer must at once be an artist and a craftsperson, recognising in modern abstraction the basic, forms which were akin to the rational requirements of mass-production. This suggests his meaning in the phrase

"simplicity IN MULTIPLICITY"

Among the aesthetic discourses addressed at the Dessau Bauhaus was that between emerging modernism, primary form and contemporary graphic design. Here Moholy-Nagy's influence as both a pedagogue and a designer was considerable. After his arrival in 1922 he assumed responsibility for the metalworking shop and, along with Herbert Bayer, was responsible for engineering a new philosophy of graphic design. In 1925, Bayer, a former student at Weimar under Kandinsky, was appointed the new director of innovative advertising workshops. Under their direction, Bauhaus graphics became more insistent upon formal geometricism, expressing a hard-edged, machine-age aesthetic in which basic form had a far greater significance. Moholy-Nagy produced a series of Bauhaus designs including the *Bauhausverlag* letterhead and exhibition poster of 1923, and the book design for Gropius' *Bauhaus Bauten Dessau* of 1928. Each displays his consistent defiance of traditional layout formulae and a compositional reorganisation based upon a "constructive" approach. Moholy-Nagy exploited the full communicative potential of all graphic elements, including the "empty" ground. His somewhat diagrammatic method mapped out visual statements in a fully integrated graphic language comprising "modern" typeface, geometric form, ruled line, limited colour palette, and "positive" rather than negative space.

Herbert Bayer went on to teach typography at Dessau between 1925 and 1928. A fully graphic, rather than merely textual approach is equally evident in his work. In his poster design for the 1927 "Europaisches Kunstgewerbe" Exhibition the typeface performs as a thoroughly visual, as well as textual element. The geometric configurations of the letters, their consistent thickness, variety of colour and regular distribution across the surface help to emphasise the grid system of the composition and the rationalist principles which underlie Bayer's approach. Bayer incorporated photographic features into his typographical compositions, and like Moholy-Nagy, integrated a range of techniques into the school's graphic design agenda. Bayer also rejected historical lettering in favour of a strict use of a lowercase alphabet, arguing economy for the purposes of typesetting and production.

When Hannes Meyer took over as Director of the Bauhaus in 1928 he instituted an ever more extreme, albeit realistic policy towards design. He refuted any contribution of aesthetics, instead stressing the role of technology and materials. For him design was an anonymous creation of the engineer, bringing Bauhaus policy into line with an uncompromising machine aesthetic and guiding the school towards industry in a way Gropius was never able to do.

Ludwig Mies van der Rohe, the third and last of the Bauhaus directors, himself became an icon of twentieth-century design. When the school closed he emigrated directly to America while other former Bauhaus members went first to England.

During an interlude in London Gropius was associated with Jack Pritchard's Isokon design group as a consultant, while Moholy-Nagy became an art director for *Architectural Review*, and Breuer contributed designs for bent ply furniture to Isokon. His Isokon *chaise longue* was a further development of original Bauhaus ideas, and was manufactured from 1936. The piece is a paradigm of his contribution to twentieth-century furniture design in his daring exploitation of the structural and aesthetic possibilities offered by manufactured materials.

During the 1930s the United States was extremely seductive to many Europeans for artistic as well as political reasons. Moholy-Nagy emigrated to Chicago in 1936, while Gropius accepted a professorship at Harvard University and left England for Cambridge, Massachussets, in the following year. Breuer also left for America in 1937 in response to Gropius' invitation of a place on the Harvard faculty. Herbert Bayer was in America by 1938. As a result of this diaspora, the innovative work of the Bauhaus continued in the United States where architecture became the focus of a new American design agenda.

In his role as Professor of Architecture at Harvard, Gropius concentrated on teaching and was able to affect emerging generations of American architects. His belief in collaboration led to the formation in 1945 of The Architects' Collaborative, a professional practice known as "TAC". Here gifted young women and men worked alongside Gropius in a variety of design endeavours, including everything from tableware to Harvard's progressive new Graduate Centre of 1949 and New York's new Pan Am Building of 1958–63. It was in the United States that as an architect Gropius was able to both teach and demonstrate his ideas more fully and without any fear of ideological suppression.

In America, Herbert Bayer greatly furthered principles of the new Bauhaus graphics. Having successfully established himself as a graphic designer in New York, he participated in the major Bauhaus exhibition at the Museum of Modern Art for which he acted as both a designer and curator. Then in 1945 he co-ordinated an exhibition of modern advertising artwork for the Container Corporation of America becoming the company's chief design consultant thereafter.

Both Moholy-Nagy and Mies van der Rohe moved to Chicago. Mies became a Professor at the Armour Institute, later renamed the Illinois Institute of Technology, where he redesigned the school from 1939 relying on principles of Bauhaus geometry and units of the basic cube. After 1945 he designed a number of increasingly simplified structures, including the steel-framed and abstract Lake Shore Drive apartments (1951) in Chicago, and the Seagram Building (1958) in New York. Like Gropius, who after 1945 designed for Rosenthal in Selb, Mies contributed to Germany's post-war architectural programme with the new National Gallery in Berlin from 1963 onwards, a further variation on the glass-walled "pavilion".

Although the Bauhaus was subject to both internal and external upheaval, and altered its orientation on more that one occasion, until its inception there had been no art and design school of its type. Its curriculum was extremely progressive and experimental. Its historical reputation in large part now rests upon the methods of design education first developed there, while much of its recent re-evaluation has centred upon both claims and refutations that its method of education was specifically suited to the requirements of industrial design. Whether or not the school's policy or its individual practitioners achieved their stated aims, its impact was enormous.

Haussuchung im „Bauhaus Steglitz"
Kommunistisches Material gefunden.

Auf Veranlassung der Dessauer Staatsanwaltschaft wurde gestern nachmittag eine größere Aktion im „Bauhaus Steglitz", dem früheren Dessauer Bauhaus, in der Birkbuschstraße in Steglitz durchgeführt. Von einem Aufgebot Schutz-

war jedoch verschwunden, und man vermutete, daß sie von der Bauhausleitung mit nach Berlin genommen worden waren. Die Dessauer Staatsanwaltschaft setzte sich jetzt mit der Berliner Polizei in Verbindung und bat um Durch-

Alle Anwesenden, die sich nicht ausweisen konnten, wurden zur Feststellung ihrer Personalien ins Polizeipräsidium gebracht.

polizei und Hilfspolizisten wurde das Grundstück besetzt und systematisch durchsucht. Mehrere Kisten mit illegalen Druckschriften wurden beschlagnahmt. Die Aktion stand unter Leitung von Polizeimajor Schmahl.

Das „Bauhaus Dessau" war vor etwa Jahresfrist nach Berlin übergesiedelt. Damals waren bereits von der Dessauer Polizei zahlreiche verbotene Schriften beschlagnahmt worden. Ein Teil der von der Polizei versiegelten Kisten

suchung des Gebäudes. Das Bauhaus, das früher unter Leitung von Professor Gropius stand, der sich jetzt in Rußland aufhält, hat in einer leerstehenden Fabrikbaracke in der Birkbuschstraße in Steglitz Quartier genommen. Der augenblickliche Leiter hat es aber vor wenigen Tagen vorgezogen, nach Paris überzusiedeln. Bei der gestrigen Haussuchung wurde zahlreiches illegales Propagandamaterial der KPD. gefunden und beschlagnahmt.

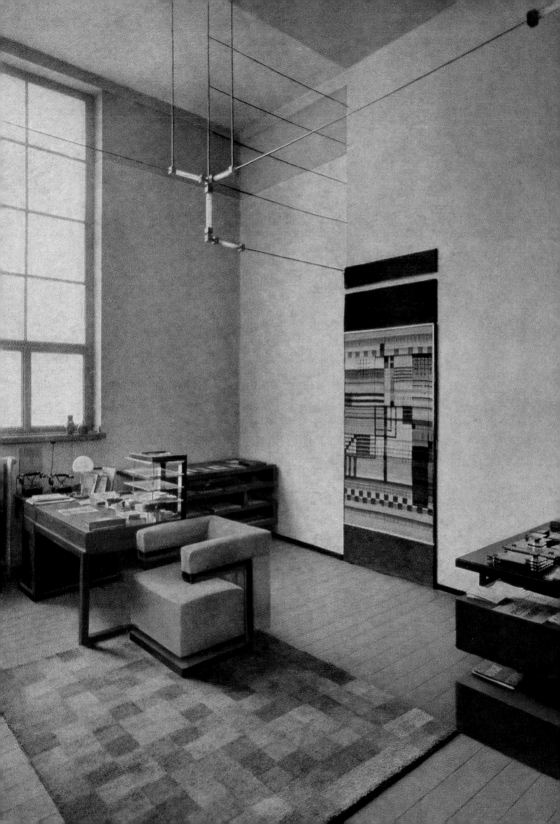

STAATLICHES

BAUHAUS

WEIMAR

1919
1923

WEIMAR-MÜNCHEN

BAUHAUSVERLAG

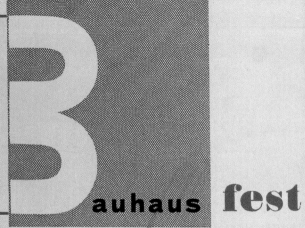

rennend
boxend
radelnd
pustend
schnaufend
grillen treibend
fliegen fangend
böcke schießend
hoffend
harrend

**so verbringt ihr
eure kurzen tage
bis zum**

Bauhaus **fest**

ge malt
ge scheckt
ge fleckt
ge putzt
ge schniegelt
ge bügelt
ge pudert
wir erwarten sie ge schminkt

am 1. märz

BAUHAUSVERLAG G.M

**GESCHÄFTSSTELLE
MÜNCHEN**

BAUHAUSVERLAG

MÜNCHEN
Wormserstraße1

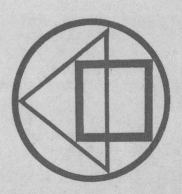

BAUHAUS
BÜCHER

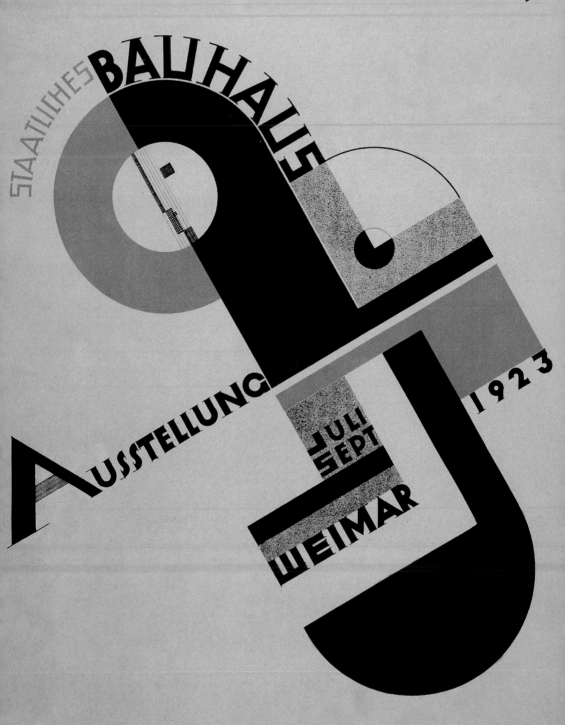

ANHALTISCHER
KUNSTVEREIN
JOHANNISSTR. 13

GEMÄLDE AQUARELLE

KANDINSKY

JUBILÄUMS-AUSSTELLUNG

zum

60.
GEBURTSTAG

Geöffnet:	Wochentags: 2 - 5 nachm.
	Mittwoch u. Sonntag 11 -1
Eintritt:	Mitglieder: Frei
	Nichtmitglieder: 50 Pfg.

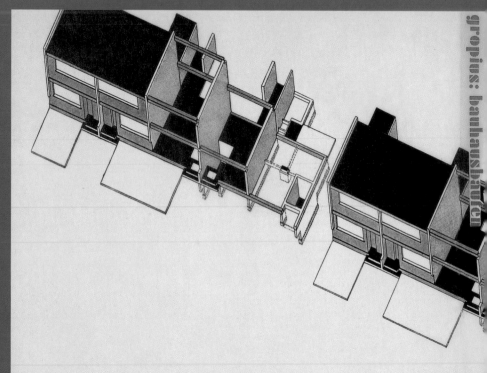

gropius: bauhausbauten

12

ALBERT LANGEN VERLAG / MÜNCHEN

bauhausbücher

12

gropius
bauhaus
bauten
dessau

band 1
der
bauhausbücher

groplus:

**internationale
architektur**

sechste auflage
broschlert rm 5
in leinen
gebunden rm 7

BAUHAUSDessau g. Stöbel

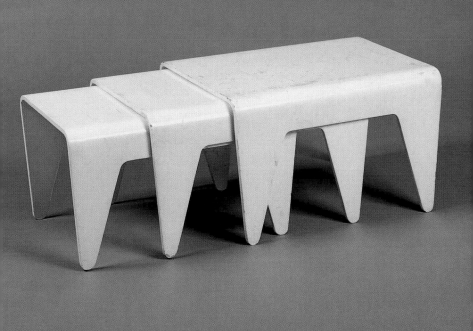

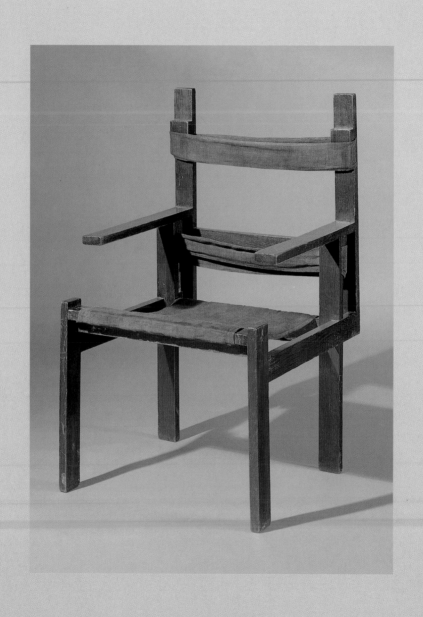

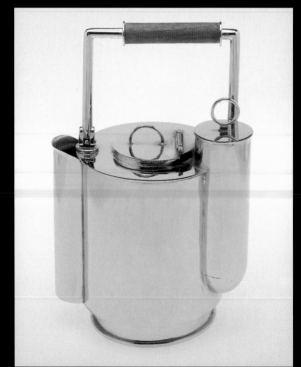

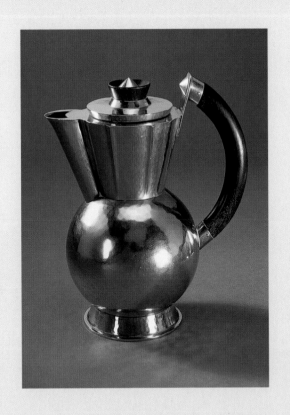

BAUHAUS BUILDING

Cantilevered balconies of the student accommodation block, Bauhaus building, Dessau, 1925–26, Walter Gropius.

WORKSHOP

Carpentry workshop at the Weimar Bauhaus, 1923.

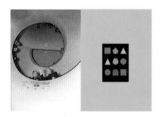

GROPIUS AND MOHOLY-NAGY/BATZ

Left: Walter Gropius and László Moholy-Nagy accompanied by students. Right: Eugen Batz, 1929–30, exercise in "ordering" forms and colours from Kandinsky's seminar on colour; tempera.

WASSILY CHAIR

Designed by Marcel Breuer, 1925.

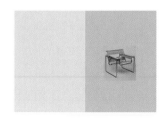

FAGUS SHOE FACTORY

1910–11, Walter Gropius and Adolph Meyer, Alfeld-an-der-Leine, the image shows the workshops of the main wing.

STUDENTS/LE CORBUSIER

Left: Students gathered outside the Bauhaus workshop building, Weimar 1920. Right: Walter Gropius meeting with Le Corbusier in a Paris café in 1923.

BAUHAUS "MASTERS"

Left: clockwise from top left, Gerhard Marcks, Walter Gropius. Mies van der Rohe, Marcel Breuer. Right, above the Masters at the Dessau Bauhaus, 1926; from left to right: Albers, Scheper, Muche, Moholy-Nagy, Bayer, Schmidt, Gropius, Breuer, Kandinsky, Klee, Feininger, Stölzl, Schlemmer.

BAUHAUS DESSAU

Workshop wing of the Bauhaus, Dessau.

BAUHAUS DESSAU

Left: Walter Gropius, Bauhaus building, Dessau, 1925–26. Right: Side view of student apartments.

GLASS

Glass curtain walls reveal the work spaces inside, Bauhaus building, Dessau.

INTERIOR

Left: Bauhaus Canteen.

Right: view from the inside of the curtain walls.

DIRECTOR'S HOUSE

Director's House, Bauhaus, Dessau, 1926, designed by Walter Gropius.

DIRECTOR'S HOUSE

Interior of the Director's Room at the Weimar Bauhaus, 1923, including furniture designed by Marcel Breuer and other artefacts designed and produced in the Bauhaus workshops.

GRAPHICS

Left: title page for the *Staatliches Bauhuas Weimar* 1919–23, dersigned by László Moholy-Nagy, 1923. Right: Postcard invitation to the Bauhaus Carnival, designed by Franz Ehilich.

LAZLO MOHOLY-NAGY

Examples of Moholy-Nagy's graphic work: a sheet of writing paper and envelope with the Bauhaus Verlag Letterhead, 1923 (left). Right: Prospectus cover advertising the Bauhaus Book series, 1924.

POSTERS

Left: Joost Schmidt, poster for the 1923 Weimar Bauhaus Exhibition entitled "Art & Technology", 1922–23, lithograph. Right: Herbert Bayer, 1926 poster for the "Kandinsky 60th Birthday Exhibiton" at Dessau.

GRAPHICS

Left: Herbert Bayer, title page for the journal *bauhaus*, 1928, letterpress. Right: Theo Ballmer, Typographical Collage *Arbeit* c.1929 from the Dessau Bauhaus.

BOOK DESIGN

Book cover design for the *Bauhaus Book* by Lázló Moholy-Nagy, 1928.

GUNTA STÖZL

Examples of the work of Gunta Stölzl: wallhanging of 1927–28, made at the Bauhaus weaving workshop, Dessau, from cotton, wool, linen and silk (left). Right: textile design in watercolour, c. 1927, for the Dessau Bauhaus.

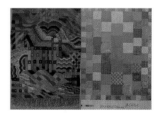

STEEL CHAIR

Ludwig Mies van der Rohe, chromium plated tubular steel chair with caning, 1927.

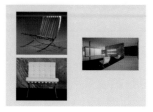

FURNITURE

Views of Mies van der Rohe's so-called "Barcelona" chair, 1929, the chair was made of chrome-plated steel and leather.

MARCEL BREUER

Left: nesting tables, c.1925–30, for Thonet and Standard Möbel. Right: nest of stacking side tables for the Isokon Furniture Co., London, laminated plywood, c.1935. Both by Breuer.

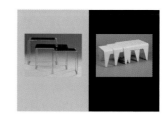

CHAIRS

Left:lounge chair of 1928–29, and table of the 1930s for Thonet, by Breuer. Right: Ludwig Mies van der Rohe, "MR" chair, 1927, manufactured by Thonet 1933–35.

MARCEL BREUER

Left: chaise-longue for Isokon, 1935–36, made from laminated birch and plywood. Right: the "Wassily" armchair, 1925, made from chrome-plated tubular steel.

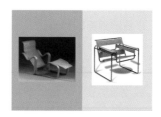

ERICH DIECKMANN

Left: sideboard, made by Erich Dieckmann, c.1926. Right: dining room table and chairs, also by Dieckmann.

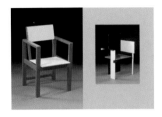

CHAIRS

Left: a child's chair, designed by Dieckmann, c.1928. Right: the "Berlin" chair, designed 1923 by Gerit Reitveld.

CHAIRS

Both by Marcel Breuer. A 1924 armchair (left) produced in the Weimar Bauhaus cabinetmaking workshop and constructed from oak with canvas upholstery. Right: tubular steel adjustable swivel chair, manufactured 1927–28 by Standard Möbel.

LIGHTING

Left: Karl Jucker and Wilhelm Wagenfeld, table lamp of 1923–24, made in the Weimar Bauhaus metal workshop, glass, nickel-plated brass and steel. Right: Marianne Brandt and Hin Bredensieck, Kandem night light, 1928.

TABLEWARE

Clockwise from left to right: pitcher made by Theodor Bogler at the Bauhaus ceramics workshop, c.1922, with a pitcher and cocoa pot by Otto Lindig; wine jug and lid by Christian Dell, 1922; teapot by Marianne Brandt, 1924; teamaker by Wolfgang Timpel, 1927.

TEA SERVICE

The Architects' Collaborative, "TAC 1" Tea Service for the Rosenthal Studio-Linie, 1969, designed by De Sousa and McMillen.

Picture credits

The publishers would like to thank the following sources for their kind
permission to reproduce the pictures in this book:

Special thanks to Sabine Hartmann, Fotoarchiv at the Bauhaus-Archiv, Museum für
Gestaltung, Berlin.

Every effort has been made to acknowledge correctly and contact the source
and/copyright holder of each picture, and Carlton Books Limited apologizes for any
unintentional errors or omissions which will be corrected in future editions of this book.

Bibliography

Hans Wingler, *Das Bauhaus* (Cologne, 1962)

Frank Whitford, *Bauhaus* (London, 1984)

Gillian Naylor, *The Bauhaus Reassessed*, sources and design theory (London, 1985)

Sigrid Wortmann Weltge, *Bauhaus Textiles, women artists and the weaving workshop*

(London, 1993)